THE BOOK OF QUESTIONS

Gregory Stock, Ph.D.

Workman Publishing • New York

TO MOM AND DAD,

*who gave me the security to question and the
independence to seek my own answers*

AND TO SADIE,

*whose questions and answers have helped me
see the world with young eyes again*

———————————

Library of Congress Cataloging-in-Publication Data is available.

ISBN 978-0-7611-7731-9

Workman books are available at special discounts when purchased in bulk for
premiums and sales promotions as well as for fund-raising or educational use.
Special editions or book excerpts can also be created to specification.
For details, contact the Special Sales Director at the address below or
send an email to specialsales@workman.com.

Design by Becky Terhune

Workman Publishing Co., Inc.
225 Varick Street
New York, NY 10014-4381
workman.com

WORKMAN is a registered trademark of Workman Publishing Co., Inc.

Printed in the United States of America
First printing September 2013

10 9 8 7 6

INTRODUCTION AND REFLECTIONS ON THE NEW EDITION

I still recall my first experiences with some of these questions 25 years ago: passing interactions in cafés that turned into delightful tête-à-têtes; conversations with old friends that brought me unexpected insights; tepid evenings that came alive and lasted into the wee hours.

When *The Book of Questions* was first released, it was 1987: Ronald Reagan and Mikhail Gorbachev were in office. The Berlin Wall was standing. Whites ruled South Africa. Prozac had just been released. Bruce Springsteen's *Tunnel of Love* topped the charts. *The Bill Cosby Show* was heading the TV ratings. Digital cameras, the Web, and the Human Genome Project didn't exist. The World Trade Center still thrust 107 stories into the New

York skyline. And a good mobile phone cost $2,500, weighed 2 pounds, and had to be charged after an hour of talking at fifty cents a minute.

Everything was different. And nothing was different. People struggled then as they do now with money and family, love and loss, hope and fear. They grappled with illness, death, failure, and frustration. They sought meaning and fulfillment. They knew temptation and betrayal. They struggled, as we still do, to carve a place in the world and to understand themselves and others.

The time was ripe for questions not about trivia, but about values and beliefs, and *The Book of Questions* provided them through simple, original, concrete, accessible dilemmas to tickle our minds and probe our thinking about core issues: life, love, money, sex, integrity, generosity, pride, death.

The book struck a chord, and the first edition was translated into 18 languages, sold more than two and a half million copies, gave rise to a whole genre of question books, and earned a special place in many people's hearts.

Today, the central challenges of life have not changed, but culture has. Context has. Language and focus have. This new edition is more than a cosmetic scrubbing of dated phrasings and references; it's a fresh new book with over a hundred new questions that infuse current technology and society into age-old dilemmas.

The questions still jump from subject to subject, so even if you read them in order, you'll face unexpected issues and topics. Pay attention to which ones you're drawn to and which you shy away from. We react to questions that touch issues that are unresolved for us, so a question you want to avoid might be the very one you should focus on. Are you fascinated by questions about health and mortality? Do you skip questions with a sexual slant? Why?

Too often we exchange small talk without really engaging one another. Try the questions here with some friends or strangers, and see what happens. You may be pleasantly surprised. And when you go off on tangents, allow yourself to voice some of those dangerous questions that you usually hold back—those flitting, provocative thoughts whispered by an inner voice. Sure they may be a bit awkward or intrusive, but often they're the very ones that open new paths to intimacy and understanding. Life can be juicy and engaging when we're grappling with issues we really care about.

Remember, though, that these questions have no correct or incorrect answers, only honest or dishonest ones. Can you truly know what you would do with some magical power or in a strange hypothetical situation? Of course not. But why let that stop you? Here you can learn and gain insights without actually living through the predicaments described. So let yourself be swept up in these situations. Try to care about the choices you make. Resist the temptation to escape dilemmas by denying their reality or by finding complications that obscure them.

Suspend your disbelief if you can. Ignore the paradoxes of time travel, the limits of our knowledge, the impossibility of magical powers. Accept that conditions are as the questions describe, that odds are accurate, that promises will be fulfilled, and that you know all of this when you make your decisions.

Push beyond a simple "yes" or "no." Probe and explain your responses. Look into your heart, be honest and brave, and let your mind really play with the difficult choices you find. If you do, these questions will lead you into some intriguing, unexpected, rewarding, even life-changing discussions and explorations. And please pursue any interesting tangents that come to mind: These questions are meant as a point of departure, not a destination.

The more you engage with them, the more they will bring you. So give your imagination free rein and take an active role in toying with the conditions: Expand, adjust, and shift them to make your choices richer and even harder. And who knows? As you explore and challenge your values and those of your friends, you may find (as I have) that questioning can be more than an entertaining pastime: It can become a way of life.

THE
BOOK of
QUESTIONS

001

Technology has become a part of us. Would you rather lose the use of all motorized vehicles, all telecommunication devices and computers, or one of your hands?

002

What would you do if your 6-year-old daughter's favorite toy, a talking doll, started trying to convince her that she needed a new friend—the next doll in the company's line?

003

If you had to be obsessed with money, sex, sports, religion, or food, which one would you choose?

004

Ignoring all financial considerations, would you rather spend the next 5 years confined to an urban mecca like New York City, or a beautiful, isolated town on the California coast?

005

Would you rather watch an Olympics that outlawed performance-enhancing drugs or one that embraced them and let athletes use medical pit crews to jack up their performances?

006

How would you react if you learned that a sad and beautiful poem that touched you deeply had been written by a computer?

How would you feel if you knew that within a century, intelligent machines would be self-aware and much smarter and more creative than humans? Why?

007

What is the most serious law you've broken doing something you thought was morally right, wouldn't hurt anyone, or was no one's business but yours? How bad would the punishment have been if you'd been caught and given the maximum sentence?

■ If you were on a jury, would you be willing to convict a person for something you didn't think should be considered a crime?

008

If you could anonymously and safely destroy any one person's reputation online through various postings, would you? If so, who and why?

On a typical Sunday, 10,000 people visit the Louvre in Paris. If a wicked sorcerer threatened to vaporize all the museum's visitors or all of its art, sparing one or the other based on your plea, which would you save? Assume the sorcerer will obliterate both the people and the art if you don't choose.

■ What, if any, fruits of our culture are worth more than even a million lives? For example, what if all the music or fiction of the past century was at risk?

010

If your heart were damaged beyond repair, but you could regain your health for a few more years by getting a heart transplant from a genetically engineered pig, would you?

011

Would you like there to be a law requiring the police to archive video footage of everything they do while on duty?

012

For $100,000, would you put on 40 pounds and keep it on for 3 years? How much money, if any, would induce you to put on 100 pounds for at least a year?

If it were the only way you could remain with the love of your life, would you be willing for both of you to wake up tomorrow as native speakers of an unfamiliar foreign language, knowing that within a week you'd permanently forget the languages you now speak and largely be cut off from your friends and culture? If so, what new language would you want to speak, and why?

014

If the person you were engaged to was in a car crash and became a paraplegic, would you back out of the marriage? If not, what if they became a quadriplegic?

■ What if you found that the person you planned to marry would likely get Alzheimer's by his or her 50th birthday?

015

Would you like to be famous? If so, for what? What if you knew it meant that within a few years you'd lose all your current friends and never develop new relationships that were as meaningful?

016

If women were just fundamentally smarter and harder working than men, would you support putting rules in place to ensure that men would share equally in the best jobs and fill half the slots at the best schools? If so, how would you explain the fairness of this to a smart, dedicated woman displaced by a less-qualified man?

017

If, without being detected, you could spy electronically for the next month and watch anyone, anywhere, anytime like a fly on a wall, would you? If so, who would you watch and how closely? If not, why not?

■ What if they might someday find out you'd been watching? Do you think you could ever be at ease under constant surveillance?

018

If your mother and father told you that they never really loved or even liked you, and you knew it was absolutely true, how would it affect your life? What if you simply over-heard them saying this to someone else?

■ Have you ever told anyone that you didn't like or love your parents?

019

If a crystal ball could tell you the truth about any one thing about yourself, life, the future, or anything else, what would you want to know, and why?

If ads could be tailored so effectively to your personal desires and concerns that they'd be nearly irresistible, would you want to ban them? Would you buy special high-tech sunglasses that screened out billboards and other advertising to leave a pristine visual landscape?

021

If evidence of intelligent life elsewhere in the universe were discovered, would it alter your core beliefs or sense of self?

■ What if instead it demonstrated that we were the only intelligent life in the galaxy?

022

If you could legally pay whatever income tax you wanted, what fraction of your earnings would you give the government? If you knew that everyone would have to pay that exact same fraction of their incomes, would you choose any differently?

■ What fraction of what you currently own would you give to the government if you knew that everyone else would have to give the same?

To be financially secure, do you work harder at anticipating risks so you can avoid them, or at building a cushion so you can withstand the unexpected? Which do you think might work better and why?

024

Would you completely rewrite your child's college application essays if it would help them get into a better school?

■ If you did help them, how would you explain to them the difference between this and cheating?

Would you like to have a high-definition nude image of yourself in your physical prime? If not, do you think you might someday wish you could see one?

You meet someone at a party and absolutely know that if you talk to him, he'll make you tens of millions of dollars, but after 2 years you'll go bankrupt and have to scramble to get back on your feet. Would you start the conversation? Assume that if you do, your knowledge of what's in store for you will vanish.

Would you like to be truly brilliant—more intelligent than 99.9 percent of the population? If so, would it matter if being that smart would virtually eliminate your sense of humor about the things that amuse most people?

028

A large crew is being chosen for an interstellar journey to a distant planet containing the first known extraterrestrial life. The expedition won't return for a century, but the crew will be in suspended animation and age only a few years during the trip. Would you be interested? If not, what, if anything, would change your mind?

Would you steal money from someone wealthy if you could get away with it and thought it was the only way to support your family?

■ What fraction of people in the world do you think would view you as wealthy?

030

What do you feel more often: gratitude or envy? What are you most grateful for?

How frequently do you express gratitude about your life?

If you were locked in a time machine set for a single one-way trip to the past or future and had 10 minutes to dial in the time and place, when and where would you go? Why? What if it were to be a round trip that would include any family and friends you wanted to bring along and safely return everyone in a week?

032

If a country hit the U.S. with a nuclear bomb, would you favor unleashing our nuclear arsenal upon them?

■ Terrorists operating out of a country that tacitly supported them kill 2 million people by setting off a nuclear bomb in downtown Chicago. Would you favor retaliating against that country, and if so, how?

Would you want to spend a week as someone of the opposite sex? someone very old? very beautiful? very ugly? or severely handicapped? If so, which one would most intrigue you?

034

If all online interactions and Web browsing had to be under your real name and would be recorded and archived, how would it alter your use of the Internet and the way you communicate with people?

Would you like your partner to be much smarter and much more attractive than you? If so, what is it about you that might hold his or her interest and love?

If you were to die this evening with no opportunity to communicate with anyone, what would you most regret not having told someone? What good might come out of telling them now?

037

You're on an airplane talking pleasantly to a stranger of average appearance. Unexpectedly, the person offers you $30,000 for one night of sex. If you knew there were no danger and you'd get the money, would you do it? If the payment were meaningfully raised or lowered, at what point would you change your answer?

How would the age and gender of the person affect your answer? What is the difference between having sex for immediate cash and having sex in the hope of other future benefits?

For $30,000 would you go for 2 months without washing, brushing your teeth, shampooing, or even using deodorant? Assume you can't tell anyone why.

■ Which would disturb you more: forgoing basic hygiene for months or having sex with a stranger?

039

If a new medicine would cure arthritis but kill 1 out of 100 people who took it, would you want it to be legal? What about a vaccine that would kill 1 in 20, but keep the others from getting cancer?

You discover that, because of a mix-up at the hospital, your wonderful 2-year-old is not actually yours. Would you want to switch kids to try to correct the mistake? Assume you'd have no further contact with the child you gave up.

041

If you knew it would completely estrange you from your friends and family, would you follow your heart and marry a person you loved?

042

Do you think the world will be a better or a worse place 100 years from now? Do you see our present world as a better place than the world of a century ago? How so?

043

Which sex has it easier in our culture? Have you ever wished you were the opposite sex?

Amnesia comes in two forms: one in which you lose your memory of past events, another in which you no longer form new memories. If you took a bad fall and were to suffer one or the other, which would be worse?

045

If you could kill people simply by imagining their deaths and saying the word "good-bye," would you use the power? Assume they'd die a natural death and no one would suspect you.

046

Would you be happier with more control over what happens in your life or more control over your response to what happens? How could you gain more such control?

047

Do you think that high-tech goggles that let you "see through" people's clothing should be banned? How much would you pay for glasses that rendered people naked?

048

Would you rather be very successful professionally with only a tolerable private life, or have a great private life but an uninspiring professional one?

If you feel your private life is more important to you, do your priorities reflect this? If not, why not?

049

What is the most outrageous thing you've ever done? Do you look back on it more with pleasure or regret?

■ Do you wish you'd been more or less cautious in your life?

If it would have no negative impact on people's health, would you render everyone in the world sterile except during months in which they took a cheap, readily available "fertility" pill? How much do you think birth rates would drop if conceiving a child required such a deliberate act?

If you could gain any one ability or quality you admire in someone else, what would you choose? Do you think you could develop that ability or quality just by working at it?

While walking in the park, you see a stranger and realize with absolute certainty that if you go over and introduce yourself, the two of you will fall in love more deeply than you even imagine possible. But you also know that in 6 months the person will be hit by a bus and killed. Would you go over to the person or leave? Assume you know that once you decide, you'll forget what lies ahead.

■ When it comes to love, is intensity or permanence more important to you? Would you embark on a long and wonderful love that you knew would end in painful betrayal?

053

If you could use a voodoo doll to hurt whoever you wished, would you use it on anyone? If so, who?

054

If someone threw a party for you and invited everyone who ever mattered to you, who would you be most excited about seeing? most anxious about? Why?

055

While on a trip, your spouse (or lover) spends a night with a stranger. If you knew they'd never meet again and you wouldn't otherwise find out about it, would you want your partner to tell you? If roles were reversed, would you confess what you'd done?

■ How serious would an affair need to be before you'd want and expect to be told about it? How much do you trust your lover? How much should they trust you?

Have your character and humanity been forged more by pleasure and success or by pain and disappointment?

■ If you could somehow protect your loved ones from pain and failure, do you think they might ultimately end up diminished by your efforts?

057

If you had to either change professions or move to another part of the country, which would you prefer? What new career or location first comes to mind?

Is the idea of being forced into such a change appealing in any way?

058

Are there people you envy so much that you'd actually want to trade lives with them? If so, who?

■ Do you think many people would want to trade lives with you if they knew your whole story? Why?

For an all-expenses-paid, one-week vacation anywhere in the world, would you be willing to tear the wings off a beautiful butterfly? If so, would you be troubled enough to enjoy your trip any less? What about stepping on a cockroach?

■ Does a beautiful creature merit more compassion than an ugly one? If so, why? Do you injure yourself psychologically by destroying something you find beautiful? Is there a meaningful difference between pulling the wings off an insect and stepping on it? How much would it take to induce you to rip the wings off a hummingbird or dove?

060

If you wanted to take a new and uncertain path in your life, but your friends really didn't want you to, would you go ahead against their wishes if you thought it was right for you?

If you were a role model to millions of children who closely followed you and your life choices, how would you change your behavior? What if only your own kids were noticing you and being affected?

062

Would you be willing to murder an innocent child to end hunger in the world? If so, what if the child had to be yours?

■ What if you had to torture the child to death to save those millions from hunger?

■ What do you think of people who achieve great things by deeply compromising their values?

063

If God appeared to you in a series of vivid and moving dreams and told you to leave everything behind, travel alone to the Sea of Galilee, and become a fisherman, would you?

■ What if God told you to kill your child to demonstrate your faith? Or to be fruitful and have as many kids as you could?

If you could have free, unlimited service for 5 years from an extremely good cook, chauffeur, housekeeper, masseuse, or personal secretary, which would you choose?

065

If a very close friend learned she had incurable cancer and only 6 months to live, would you withdraw or try to spend more time with her?

■ If you found that you had only 6 months to live, but wouldn't look ill until near the end, how long would you wait to tell family? friends? acquaintances?

066

What is your greatest accomplishment? Has it meant as much to you as you thought it would? Is there anything you hope to do that would be even better?

If your family lived in a low-lying area like New Orleans or Miami Beach, how might it change any of your lives if you knew global warming would raise sea levels a foot each century and submerge the entire place in a few hundred years?

068

Would you give up half of what you own for a pill that would permanently alter you so that sleeping an hour a day would fully refresh you without side effects?

■ Do you feel you have enough time? If not, what might give you that feeling? As you age, are you becoming less or more concerned about "wasting" time?

069

If you knew that devoting yourself to an all-consuming occupation—music, writing, acting, business, politics, or medicine—for 20 years would make you one of the best in the world at it, would you? If so, which would you choose?

If you knew that such laser focus would give you a shot at success, but no guarantee, would you still go for it?

070

What was your best experience with drugs
or alcohol? your worst?

Would you want to implant a rice grain–sized computer chip in your fingertip to enable you to throw away your credit cards and keys, and use a simple hand wave to make a purchase and unlock doors?

072

What could someone figure out about you
by the friends you've chosen?

■ Do your close friends tend to be older
or younger than you? less or more talented
and successful than you? Do they share
your values? ambitions? interests?

073

Would you have one of your fingers removed surgically if it somehow guaranteed you immunity from all major diseases?

074

If we lived for centuries and even very old people were healthy and youthful, would you rather have a partner who was old enough to be world-wise and experienced, or someone younger and more naïve who was seeing most things for the first time? Why?

■ Would you rather vacation somewhere new with a friend who knew the ins and outs of the place or with one who, like you, was seeing it for the first time?

If the government could use a mix of cameras, implanted sensors, and automated surveillance devices to follow every move of a paroled criminal indefinitely to prevent future wrongdoing, would you want to require this of convicted felons after their release? If so, for how long would you want to take away their privacy, and what limits would you place on their activities? If not, why not?

076

If you lived in a neighborhood where crime was commonplace and police were slow to respond, would you buy a gun?

■ If most of your neighbors owned guns legally, would you feel more protected or more at risk than you do now?

If you discovered that when you were conceived, you were one of five identical embryos and have four living identical twins, would you be more intrigued or distressed? Would you want to meet your siblings?

078

Your house, containing everything you own, catches fire; after saving your family and pets, you have time for a final dash to save something of yours. What would it be?

079

What is the most violent physical clash you've had with someone in recent years? Who came out ahead?

080

How would you react if you were to learn that your mate's previous lover wasn't the same sex as you?

■ Have you been sexually attracted to men and women? to someone in your family? to someone already in a serious relationship? If so, how did you (and they) deal with it?

081

If you had the power to go any distance into the future and return a year later with whatever knowledge you could obtain during your visit, would you? What would be the most valuable things to find out? What might they be worth to you?

082

You are offered $5 million to play a variant of Russian roulette: Before you are 10 pistols, 1 loaded. You must pick a pistol, point it at your forehead, and pull the trigger. If you walk away, you do so a multimillionaire. Would you take the shot?

083

Would you rather play a game with someone less or more skilled than you? Would your answer be different if others were watching?

How would it feel to always describe yourself as ordinary, no better or worse than most others? Would it be a relief or a disappointment to realize it was actually true?

084

If your mother were in pain, bedridden, and a few weeks from death, and she begged you to give her poison so she could take her own life, would you find a way to get it for her?

■ Should it be against the law to help a terminally ill person die? If so, why? If a person weren't dying but in profound emotional pain, should he or she be allowed to commit suicide?

If what you owned had no bearing on what people thought of you, would you spend your money differently?

Given the choice of anyone in the world, who would you want as your dinner guest? your friend? your lover? What do you seek in a friend that you don't expect from a lover?

Since being deprived of the Internet would be viewed by many as a serious punishment, do you think it is right to give Internet access to those in prison who are ostensibly being punished for a serious crime they've committed?

088

How often do you step back and reflect on where you are headed? Would less or more self-reflection be good for you?

■ Do you have any specific long-term goals? If so, which is the most important, how do you hope to reach it, and how do you think reaching it will enhance your life?

Some concierge health-care businesses will, for one up-front fee, guarantee free, world-class medical care for any future medical issues you face. How much of what you now own would you give up for such security?

090

If you walked out your door one morning and saw a bird with a broken wing huddled in a bush, what would you do? Why?

091

Terrorists send the president a message saying that unless he gives them $25 billion, they'll detonate a nuclear bomb in Manhattan. What should the president do? What would you do?

Would you feel differently if the city were El Paso or Indianapolis?

092

Would you be willing to give up sex for a year if you knew it would give you a much deeper sense of peace than you have now?

■ What would you be willing to give up to have as much wonderful sex as you desire for the next year?

093

Would you add a decade to your life if it meant taking a decade from the life of some random person? If so, would you still do it if you had to become friends with (and stay in touch with) the person?

094

A good friend pulls off a well-conceived practical joke, as only someone who really knows you could, and makes you look completely ridiculous. How would you react? Would it matter if you knew that they pulled the prank to make you see a side of yourself that you were blind to?

■ How forgiving are you when your friends let you down? Do you expect more or less generosity from them when you fall short?

095

Do you feel comfortable going to dinner or movies alone? Would you rather be by yourself in such a situation or with someone you only marginally enjoy?

If you knew you could direct medical research funds so as to find a cure for one specific disease within 15 years, but make little progress on any others, would you target a single disease? If so, which one and why?

097

If your best friend fell head over heels in love with someone you thought was deceptive and creepy, and you could use an anonymous service to get the lowdown on his or her credit, medical, and employment history; school records; parking tickets; politics; bank records; and Facebook postings, would you? If so, what kind of discovery would it take before you'd intervene to protect your friend?

■ If you knew that in-depth snooping would be commonplace within a decade and that everyone's life would be an open book for all to see, in what ways might you start to behave differently? Do you think that knowing everything about the people around you would be a good thing?

98

If you knew you were destined never to achieve anything of real importance, how would it change your goals and attitudes? What if you knew you were destined for great things but didn't know what?

■ What in your life do you think will seem most meaningful when you look back many years from now?

■ What do you think you'll regret when you look back?

99

If your parents became infirm and you had to either bring them into your home or put them in a nursing home, which would you do? What about any siblings of yours who were unable to care for themselves?

100

If a technological breakthrough could enable people to travel as quickly and cheaply across the world as they now do between adjacent cities, but at the price of 500,000 deaths a year, would you want the technology developed?

■ Had you lived in 1900 and known that cars would cause 20 million deaths in the next century, would you have wanted to halt their development? What present technologies do you think are too dangerous to develop, given that each year cars kill 500,000 people and cigarettes take 5 million?

If you were sentenced to hear one of the following all morning, every morning for the next year, which would be worst: a baby crying, someone screaming, someone cursing drunkenly, or the song "It's a Small World" played over and over and over again?

102

You and someone you love deeply are placed in separate rooms, each with a button next to you. You each know that you both will be killed unless one of you presses your button in the next 60 minutes. You also know that the first to hit the button will save the other, but immediately die. What would you do?

103

If you could travel into the past but not return, would you? Where would you go and what would you try to do if your goal was to reshape history?

How do you think today's world might be different if you were able to make such a change? Would you be surprised if the long-term consequences of your intervention were bad?

104

Would you rather die peacefully among friends at age 50, or painfully and alone at age 80?

105

When has your life changed dramatically as the result of some seemingly random influence or occurrence?

■ Do you think that living as if you control your own destiny is a good idea? Do you live that way?

If you could work half as much as you do now and keep the same pay, or work just as hard as you do now and get twice the pay, which would you choose?

While arguing with you on the phone, a close friend gets angry and hangs up. If he or she does not call back, would you call them? If so, how long would you wait?

108

Have you ever "borrowed" money (or anything else) from family or friends and not returned it? If so, why? Who has done this to you, and what were the consequences?

109

For extraordinary wealth, would you be willing to have terrifying nightmares every night for a year?

■ What would you do if you knew that unless you changed jobs and took a substantial pay cut, you'd have frequent insomnia and a terrible nightmare every few weeks?

110

Would you be willing to go to a slaughter-house and kill a cow? Do you eat meat?

111

Would you want to record everything you hear or see 24 hours a day, 7 days a week, year in, year out?

If you could easily find and replay any previous conversation or interaction, how would it affect your relationships?

If you could let someone know your every thought and feel your every feeling for a week, who, if anyone, would you be willing to open up to so completely? Do you think they'd like you less or more at the end of the week?

■ If people knew the real you—your weaknesses and failings, your strengths and successes—do you think their opinions of you would change much? What would surprise them the most?

Would you enjoy a month of solitude, all alone in an isolated, beautiful natural setting with food and shelter provided?

114

After a medical examination, your doctor calls and says you have a rare lymphatic cancer and only a month to live. A week later, she informs you that the lab test was wrong and you're perfectly healthy. Do you think the insights from having to face death this way would be worth the pain?

■ What life changes do you think a close brush with death might provoke for you?

One hot, sunny afternoon, you are crossing the parking lot of a large shopping center and see a dog locked in a car, suffering from the heat. Would you do anything about it? If so, what?

116

If it would greatly reduce crime in your community, would you be willing to have continuous video monitoring of all roads, walkways, parks, and other public spaces?

■ What about requiring everyone to carry an ID in public?

If you could end cigarette smoking by releasing a pathogen that would kill every tobacco plant in the world, would you? What—if anything—about doing this would most trouble you?

If you knew that in a year you would die of a heart attack, how would you alter your life?

If people routinely used tiny point-of-view cameras to record precisely what they saw and heard, what slices of life would you watch? Assume that countless dramatic videos of first-person experiences of everything from battles to crimes, sports, and sex would be readily available on the Internet.

Would you accept $2 million to leave the country and never set foot in it again? What would be the minimum amount to seriously tempt you to take this step?

■ If you had to flee the country tomorrow and never return, where would you go to build a new life, and why?

Child pornography carries heavy penalties. Should virtual child pornography involving consenting adults and lifelike computer-generated images, but no actual children, carry such penalties, too? If so, why?

When you recount something that has happened to you, do you typically exaggerate and embellish? If so, why?

123

How would it affect your life if you knew for certain that 500 years from now humanity would be thriving in an inspiring, amazing way? What if instead you knew human civilization would be gone, destroyed by global war or environmental disaster?

■ What would you do if you alone knew that in precisely 20 years the sun would explode and the world would end?

124

Is it hard for you to ask for help? If so, what about it bothers you the most?

■ Who would you turn to if you needed help? Why? Do you think that person would think of you if they were in a fix?

You're raising money for a charity and someone agrees to make a large contribution if you perform alone in front of a thousand people at an upcoming fundraiser. Would you agree? If so, how big a donation, if any, would you require, and what sort of act would you perform?

126

What would your funeral be like if you died tomorrow? Who would want to speak, and what would they say about you if they were being honest?

■ Do you care much about having people mourn your death?

A movement to reduce political corruption maintains that the only way to keep politicians even close to honest is to require them to always wear tiny video bugs that record their every interaction and to post them all online. Would you support such monitoring of key elected officials?

■ What kind of people would be attracted to politics given such a loss of privacy? How do you think such openness would affect lobbying? What would be your biggest concern about such transparency?

You, your closest friend, and your father are on vacation together, hiking near a remote lake. Your companions stumble upon a nest of poisonous snakes and are badly bitten. You know neither will live without an immediate, full dose of antivenom, yet you have only one dose. What would you do?

129

If your child were to be boring, stupid, or ugly, which one would you prefer? Would your choice depend on the child's gender?

If you could place yourself anywhere on a scale from 1 to 10, where 1 is having security and comfort and goals within easy reach, and 10 is taking risks, struggling, and reaching for great achievement, what number would you like to be at, and why? Where are you now?

131

Do you work harder to earn praise and recognition or to avoid criticism?

 Do you dispense more criticism or praise?

132

Would you be willing to undergo a relatively safe surgery to implant a permanent cardiac monitor that would detect the telltale signs of an impending heart attack and summon medical help before it occurred?

If you worked for the government and found that the president was committing serious crimes to bring about positive things you both believed in, would you try to expose the crimes? If so, what if you knew your reputation would be destroyed in the process?

What would you do if you were approached on a busy street by a well-dressed stranger who said he'd lost his wallet and asked apologetically if you could give him $9.85 to buy a train ticket?

■ What if instead you were approached for a handout by a haggard-looking stranger claiming to be hungry and unable to find a job?

135

If you could live to the age of 100 having either the body or the mind of a 25-year-old for the rest of your life, which would you prefer? What if you could keep your body or mind only as it is now?

■ What do you think would be hardest about living hundreds of years in a youthful state?

136

Do you strive more for security, accomplishment, success, love, power, or excitement?

137

Given one shot at a 50-50 bet that pays 10 times your wager if you win, how much would you risk? What if your chances of winning were 90 percent and the payoff were still tenfold?

138

What are your two most compulsive habits? Do you struggle to break them? If so, what would it feel like to accept them and give up on trying to change?

If you had to conduct all electronic communication with your friends and colleagues using only one of the following—phone, text, email, or social media—which would you choose and how do you think it would change your relationships?

140

If you could release viruses engineered to extinguish any three species you wished, what animals or plants would you get rid of? Are there any you'd like to wave good-bye to but wouldn't because of environmental or other concerns?

■ If you would not get rid of any species, do you think scientists should stop trying to wipe out the malaria parasite, which kills 3,000 people a day, and the tsetse fly, which spreads sleeping sickness to nearly as many?

141

What would you do if you found out that your closest friend was a heroin dealer?

142

You are driving late at night in a safe but deserted neighborhood, and a dog darts in front of your car. You slam on the brakes, but still hit the animal. Would you stop to help?

■ If you did stop and the dog was dead but had a name tag, would you call the owner?

143

Viagra was just the beginning. If there were two new drugs, one to raise your sex drive for 24 hours, the other to lower it, do you think you'd use either of them regularly—for example, increasing your sex drive for recreation and lowering it if you had work to do?

■ If you could consciously control your sex drive, do you think your life would be better or worse than it is now? If you had to permanently double or halve your partner's appetite for sex, which would you pick?

144

If by sacrificing your life you could contribute so much to humanity that you'd be honored everywhere, would you? If so, what if you knew your sacrifice would go unrecognized, and the credit would go to someone you detested?

■ Do you think your decision would change if you were older or younger than you are now?

145

If you could earn the same pay no matter what job you did, would you pursue another profession? If so, what would you choose, and why?

146

Does the fact that you've never done something before increase or decrease its appeal to you?

A psychotic online stalker fixates on you and mounts a relentless assault to ruin you through threatening emails, public postings with horrible accusations, and vile notes to your family, friends, and acquaintances. The authorities can do nothing, and everything else has failed to help. Only two options remain: learn to live with it, or pay a large sum to someone who will discreetly find and kill the person. Which would you choose?

148

How close and loving is your family? Do you feel your childhood was happier than most people's?

■ Do you think kids should be sheltered from unhappiness? What experiences from your own childhood have proved most valuable? What were the most difficult to overcome? Were they happy or unhappy experiences?

Would you be willing to give up sex for 5 years if you could have wonderful erotic dreams every night?

At a meal, some people you know start belittling a common acquaintance. Would you stand up for the person if you felt the criticisms were unjustified?

151

Would you want to have your rate of physical aging slowed so much that, barring some accident, you'd live for 1,000 years?

■ Do you think you might soon feel jaded or unable to relate to those around you? How hard would it be to know you'd outlive everyone you love?

152

In what period since you were a teenager did you have the most personal growth and change? If you wanted to have another such period, what could you do to bring it about or otherwise shake up your life?

153

If you were having difficulty on a critical test at school and could safely cheat by peeking online, would you?

■ If you saw someone cheating on a test, what would you do? Would it matter if you had (or hadn't) signed an honor code?

If you were enjoying a festive dinner at a friend's house and found a dead cockroach in your salad, what would you do?

For $50,000, would you put to sleep a healthy pet you love? How much more or less money would it take to change your answer?

■ What would you say if the pet weren't yours, but that of a child or friend who wanted your advice about what to do?

Which would be worse: having to leave the country and never return, or never being able to travel more than 150 miles from where you now live?

If you could become brilliant by having a visible scar stretching from your mouth to your ear, would you?

158

What was your most enjoyable dream? Your worst nightmare?

■ If you could script the plot for your next dream, what would the story be? What, if anything, have you learned about yourself from your dreams?

159

Would you be willing to shorten your life by a decade to become extraordinarily attractive? famous? wealthy? bright? or gifted in some other way?

160

If 100 people your age were chosen at random from your last school or workplace, how many do you think would be more satisfied with their lives than you are with yours? Why? What about 1,000 people chosen randomly from anywhere in the world?

161

Would it disturb you much if, upon your death, your body were thrown into the woods and left to rot? Why?

If you had a choice between two virtually equivalent medicines, one a chemical carefully synthesized in the laboratory, and the other an extract carefully harvested from a medicinal plant, which would you prefer and why?

Would you get a tattoo the size of a dinner plate if you knew it would somehow save the lives of a busload of innocent tourists who'd otherwise die? If so, what tattoo design and location would you select?

How many different sexual partners have you had in your life? Do you wish you'd had more or fewer? Why?

165

What is so important to you that, without it, life wouldn't be worth living? Would your answer have been any different 10 years ago?

■ Have you ever seriously considered suicide? If so, why?

Given that a woman can conceive a child long after menopause by using a frozen egg, is there an age beyond which it should be illegal for women to bear children? Why? What about men? If so, how would you punish violators?

167

If your friends and acquaintances were willing to honestly tell you what they thought of you, would you want them to? What do you think they might say?

■ How much energy do you spend trying to impress others? Does it bother you when people like you because they think you have qualities you don't actually have?

168

If you could wake up tomorrow in the body
of someone else and assume his or her life,
would you do it? If so, who would you pick?
What if you'd become the real you again in
a month? or a year?

169

Would you like the government to install extensive car and road sensors and automatically ticket anyone speeding, rolling through stop signs, or parking illegally?

■ What appeals to you most about aggressive, rigid enforcement of the law? What repels you?

If you were relatively happily married, had no kids, and met someone you knew would always bring you passionate, intoxicating love, would you leave your spouse? What if you had young children?

171

Would you use a drug that made you extraordinarily happy for 12 hours without any side effects? If not, why not? If so, what if it were addictive and you'd soon want to be happy all the time?

■ Would you ever use a happiness-producing drug that had one serious side effect: The next day, you'd remember the wonderful feelings but not what had actually happened? Do you treasure any memories that are more about how you felt than what occurred?

172

Who is the most important person in your life? What could you do to improve the relationship? Will you ever do it?

173

When you do something ridiculous, how much does it bother you to have other people notice it and laugh at you? What's the funniest thing about you?

■ When is the last time you really laughed at yourself? What was so funny?

You need to have dangerous brain surgery and must choose between two surgeons: one extremely gifted but a dishonest jerk; the other less skilled but very honest and friendly. Who would you pick? What if you were accused of a serious crime and had the same choice in attorneys?

175

Do you believe in capital punishment? Would you be willing to pull the switch to execute a man sentenced to death if you were randomly selected by the courts to do so and knew he would go free if you refused? Assume you know nothing about his crime.

176

If you could change anything about the way you were raised, what would it be?

■ In what ways will you treat your children differently from how your parents treated you? If you've already raised children and could do it again knowing what you know now, what would you change?

177

Is there something you've dreamed of doing for a long time but haven't? Why haven't you? Is it better to have dreams that may never come to pass, or to stick with those that can be readily achieved?

■ How much better would your life be if your dreams came true? What dreams have you already achieved?

178

Do you believe in God? If not, do you think you might nonetheless pray if you were in a life-threatening situation?

179

Your 12-year-old daughter hacks into a corporate database and causes $1 million worth of damage. When caught, she tearfully says it was just a prank and she had no idea she'd cause such damage. How should she be punished?

If you hiked to a remote beach and nearly everyone there were swimming nude, would you stay for a swim? If so, would you swim nude?

■ How much do you like your body? If you awoke on a warm morning and were going to laze around by yourself, how long would it be before you looked in a mirror? If you sleep in the nude, how long before you put on clothes?

181

Have you had really satisfying sex within the last 3 months? What key ingredients make sex particularly satisfying for you?

182

While out one day, you come upon your mother holding hands with someone who is obviously her lover. She sees you and races over, begging you not to say anything to your father. What would you do?

■ What if you'd discovered your father doing the cheating?

183

Someone close to you will die in a few months unless you donate one of your kidneys to them. If you knew that your chances of surviving the operation were excellent and that your life expectancy wouldn't be appreciably reduced, would you give up the organ? What if the operation were risky?

■ What if you could refuse without anyone knowing? or if the person with the failing kidney didn't want you to make the sacrifice?

You're with friends at an icy mountain lake on a warm sunny day. If you knew it'd be a harsh, bracing shock to jump in, but that later you'd be refreshed and glad you'd done it, would you take the leap?

185

Do you find it so hard to say no that you often end up doing favors you don't want to do? If so, why?

■ When you have to tell people something they won't want to hear, do you tell them directly? If not, why not?

When was the last time you stole something? Why haven't you stolen anything since? Is there anything you'd steal if you were certain you wouldn't get caught?

187

Would you rather spend a month on vacation with your parents or put in 4 weeks of uncompensated overtime at work?

Would you make a substantial sacrifice to have any of the following: your picture on a postage stamp; your statue in a park; a college named after you; a Nobel Prize?

■ How much does fame impress you?
Have you ever made a big sacrifice for
someone and kept it to yourself? Which
means more to you: knowing you've done
something amazing or being recognized
for doing it?

If your teenage son died in a freak accident, and you wanted another child, would you rather clone an identical twin of your dead son or try to have another child naturally?

■ What if you were no longer fertile and could not otherwise have your own biological child?

190

What, if anything, is too serious to be joked about? (Assume you aren't at an airport and subject to immediate arrest!)

191

When was the last time you felt real excitement and passion in your work? What about your life in general? How important is passion to you?

192

If you were handed an envelope with the date of your death inside, and you knew you could do nothing to alter your fate, would you look?

■ In what ways, if any, would knowing the date of your death help you plan your life? How many more years do you honestly believe you have left?

Do you ever spit, clean your teeth, or pick your nose in public?

194

Would you want to choose the sex of your child? What if you could safely pick other qualities: IQ, height, temperament, looks?

■ What problems might arise from having a child much brighter and more attractive than yourself?

■ Would you use a safe medical procedure to genetically alter the developing embryo if it would keep your child from being born physically or mentally disabled?

If someone you loved was brutally murdered and their killer was acquitted on a technicality, would you seek revenge?

If a close friend asked, and genuinely wanted, your opinion, but you knew he'd find it painful—for example, he's an artist and asks your honest appraisal of his artistic talent, and you think he's lousy—would you tell him the truth?

197

Do you have a favorite sexual fantasy? If so, what would you give to have it granted?

■ Have you told your partner about it?

198

What are the most important things (excluding children) you've brought into the world that would not exist without you?

199

Would you like to know your risk for an illness that has no effective treatment? Why?

An eccentric millionaire offers to donate a large sum to charity if you'll step naked from a car onto a busy downtown street and walk four blocks before getting back into the vehicle. If you knew there'd be no danger of physical abuse, how big a donation would it take to get you to do it? What if you knew your stroll would be posted online?

■ Which would be worse: being naked in public, getting spit on by strangers, arrested for shoplifting, throwing up on someone at dinner, or begging on the street?

■ If you were guaranteed anonymity, how much would it bother you to be humiliated in front of strangers you'd never see again?

Would you accept an inflation-adjusted lifetime stipend of $150,000 per year if it meant you couldn't earn or inherit additional money? What would be the lowest such stipend you'd agree to?

When did you last cry in front of another person? to yourself?

203

If you were attracted to someone of another race, in what ways, if any, would your behavior with them differ from that with someone of your own race? Why?

■ What about someone devoted to a different religion or immersed in a very different culture?

If you were given a voice-activated watch that tracked your whereabouts and would quickly summon the police if you shouted for help, would you wear it? If so, would the added safety lead you to do anything you wouldn't do now?

■ If you could use such a device to create a minute-by-minute archive of precisely where you'd been, would you? If so, what would you do with it, and would anything worry you about others getting the information?

Do you believe in ghosts or evil spirits?
Would you be willing to spend a night
alone in a remote, supposedly haunted
house?

206

Do you judge others by higher or lower standards than you judge yourself?

Many people are capable of being good runners, but to be world-class you need specific variants of key genes. If you were the best runner in your area and really wanted to win an Olympic gold medal, would you first check your genes? If so, what if you found you didn't have the right ones?

208

Would you be willing to forgo all use of the Internet for 5 years if your sacrifice meant that someone would permanently provide for 1,000 children, saving them from starvation?

■ Would you still do it if you also had to give up texting, email, phone, and TV?

■ What if instead you had to give up dessert for the rest of your life?

Which would you rather have: one inti-mate soul mate but no other good friends, or no soul mate but lots of good friends?

If you had to spend the next 2 years in a small, fully provisioned Antarctic shelter with one other person, who would you want to be with?

211

If you learned you were going to die in a few days, what regrets would you have? Which of them could you resolve if you were given another 5 years?

■ Do you try to envision your future and live now as you think you'll one day wish you had?

If your car told you in a soothing voice to watch your weight as soon as you started putting on pounds, how long would it take you to disconnect the feature?

Which would you prefer: a wild, turbulent
life filled with joy, sorrow, passion, adven-
ture, intoxicating successes, and stunning
setbacks; or a happy, secure, predictable life
surrounded by friends and family, without
wide swings of fortune and mood?

Would you accept $20,000 to shave your head and continue your normal activities without a hat or wig until your hair grew back? What is the minimum price you'd take for this?

215

If you knew that your child-to-be would be severely retarded and die by the age of 5, would you want to abort? Should fathers have any legal rights about such a decision?

■ What are your feelings about killing a severely handicapped baby at birth if the parents can't (or won't) care for him, and he'd require institutional care his entire life?

216

You become romantically involved with someone but after a couple of years realize you want out. What would you do if you were convinced that your lover would commit suicide if you left?

217

For $5,000, would you be willing to stand up in a crowded restaurant and obnoxiously berate a server about some trivial problem? If not, is it because it would embarrass you or because it would hurt her feelings?

■ Do you think a server would rather have you forgo the bet or split the money with her later?

218

Under what circumstances—if any—would you want to watch a public execution in person? What about a graphic video of it posted online?

219

If advanced technologies enabled everyone to enjoy the material benefits of an upper-middle-class lifestyle without having to work, how would you change your life? What would most concern you about such a bountiful world?

220

If someone offered you a large bribe for privileged information about one of your company's products, would you take it? Assume you knew you wouldn't be discovered.

■ How do you feel about taking a sick day when you aren't sick, or falsifying an expense report? If an ATM gave you extra cash, would you report the error?

221

If you could take a one-month trip anywhere in the world and money were not a consideration, where would you go and what would you do?

Would you want every person in the country to have genetic information saved in a DNA databank so that small genetic readers could accurately ID anyone at anytime? What would be your biggest concern about such a system?

223

Would you do something boring and unsatisfying (say, cleaning toilets) for 5 years if you knew it would bring you contentment and inner peace for the rest of your life? If not, how long would you be willing to do it?

224

Would you be willing to become physically ugly if it meant you could live for 100 more years at your current physical age?

■ How much do you think it would change your life if you were in an accident that left your face permanently disfigured?

225

Would you choose to escape death if you could do so by having your brain removed from your dying body, suspended in nutrients, and wired to sensors and controllers that let you see, hear, and speak? Do you find this idea more horrifying or intriguing? Why?

■ What if you could be seamlessly linked into all online communication paths, social-media applications, and games, so that you'd effectively be living online?

226

Is there anything in your life too personal to discuss with others? If so, have you ever made the mistake of trying? What happened?

227

While walking, you come upon a lost wallet containing $1,000. Would you return it if there were a name and address inside? Would you act differently if the person's photo ID showed a wealthy-looking young man or a frail-looking old woman?

■ If you lost your own purse or wallet, do you think there is much of a chance that someone would return it to you?

If you were fated to be in a bad accident that would leave you either blind, deaf, or with amnesia that wiped away all your memories, which loss would be the worst? the easiest?

If you had a child who was your clone—a delayed identical twin—do you think that your hard-won self-awareness and self-knowledge would enable you to be a better parent for him or her than your parents were for you?

230

Could a marriage of the highest quality in all respects but one—it completely lacked sex—be satisfying to you?

■ Are you able to separate sex from love? Could you be content for long satisfying your sexual needs with people other than your mate?

231

Would you be willing to eat a bowl of live crickets for $5,000? What is the least amount of money you'd take to do this?

The night before you fly off on a family vacation, you get a reading from a fortune teller at a party. In the middle of it, the psychic gets very upset and says she sees a plane bursting into flames and you burning and screaming. Would you be disturbed enough to change your travel plans?

233

Do you think you have much impact on the lives of people whose paths you cross? Has anyone, over a short period of time, significantly influenced your life?

■ Does advice from older people carry any special weight for you because of their greater experience?

A deaf couple plans to have a baby by IVF so they can implant an embryo with genes that will ensure that their child will be deaf. Do you think this is wrong? Should it be illegal?

235

Would you rather have success and everything material you want, but few friends; or little success or material well-being, but lots of friends?

If you could give anyone a love potion that would so open their heart to you that they'd be hopelessly in love with you forever, would you? If so, who? Do you think the responsibility of their devotion might ever become a burden to you?

■ Have you ever wished you could be in love with someone you merely liked? Would you be tempted to take a pill that would make you fall in love with a person who seemed right for you, even if there were no guarantee your love would be returned?

237

If you could reshape your recollections of any unpleasant past experience and replace your present memories with ones much more palatable, would you? If so, what would you change, and why?

■ If a wonderful, now-dead relative had actually been a child molester, or your fondly remembered, now-departed father had been a thief and a fraud, would you want to know? If so, why?

238

Have you ever disliked someone for being luckier or more successful than you?

239

How old were you when you first had sex? Do you think you'd have been better off if you had waited longer or started earlier?

■ Is there anything anyone could have told you that would have improved your first sexual experience?

240

What do you like best about your life? least?

241

If you were given $1 million to donate anonymously to a stranger or cause of your choice, how would you dispose of it?

Would you rather live in a country where people can get rich if they succeed in business but might wind up destitute if they fail, or in a place where there is little opportunity to achieve wealth but a strong social safety net in place?

243

You are leading 100 people whose lives are in danger, and you must pick one of two paths. One will save 95 people but 5 will die; the other has an even chance of saving everyone, but if it fails everyone will die. Which would you choose?

■ If you had to choose the 5 people who'd die, how would you do it?

244

What would you do if you found your 13-year-old child looking at shocking hard-core pornography on the Internet?

245

If you could take a pill and eat food all day without absorbing calories or nutrition, would you? If so, is there any particular food you'd gorge on?

246

If you were having a child by IVF and could safely add 25 years to your kid's life expectancy by injecting an artificial chromosome into the embryo, would you?

■ Would you feel more pleased or disappointed to learn that your parents could have used genetic engineering to enhance your health and increase your life expectancy, but decided to keep you "natural" and unenhanced? What if half the people you knew were genetically enhanced?

247

Would you rather be given $25,000 for your own use or $250,000 to give anonymously to strangers? What if you could either keep $5 million or give away $50 million?

248

How many of your friendships have lasted more than 10 years? Which of your friends do you think will still be important to you a decade from now?

A cave-in occurs while you and an acquaintance are exploring a concrete armory deep beneath the ground in an old converted mine shaft. You learn that the entire shaft is now sealed and an airhole being drilled won't reach you for 15 hours. If you both take sleeping pills from a medicine chest to slow your metabolism, the oxygen will still last only 10 hours. There's no way for you both to survive, but one of you probably could. What would you do if the other person took a sleeping pill, motioned toward a loaded pistol, said it was up to you, and nodded off?

250

What sorts of things would you do if you could be as outgoing and uninhibited as you wished?

■ Do you usually initiate friendships or wait to be approached?

251

To prevent the otherwise certain extinction of the blue whale, what would be the longest time you'd be willing to spend as a quadriplegic, paralyzed below the neck? Assume that a complete recovery would be instantaneous.

■ What is so precious to you that you'd never sacrifice it for anything? your integrity? your health? your happiness? your child?

252

Do you seek or avoid routines in your life, for instance, sleeping in the same part of your bed? ordering the same meals? returning to the same vacation spots? Why?

253

Would you rather be happy but slow-witted and unimaginative, or unhappy yet bright and creative? For example, would you choose the life of a tortured, brilliant artist like Vincent van Gogh, or of a happy, carefree, simpleminded soul?

254

Can you be counted on to do what you say you'll do? What does it take for you to trust someone?

255

Would you rather live nearer to your parents or farther away from them? What about your brothers, sisters, or grown children?

256

When you are with your friends, do your interactions include much hugging, kissing, roughhousing, rubbing backs, and such? Would you like to have less or more of such touching?

257

If you could travel into the future but not return, would you? What if you could take along a few companions? If you had to make the trip, how far forward would you go?

■ What would induce you to give up life as you know it and face the unknown?

■ Do you think people in previous centuries were more adventurous than we are or simply more used to risk?

258

Of all the people close to you, whose death would disturb you most?

259

Would you want your child's elementary school to have hundreds of hidden cameras monitoring everything going on, so that parents could go online anytime to watch their kids?

■ Do you think having such video records would be a good educational tool if used to replay select occurrences and disputes so children could watch themselves in real situations and discuss what happened?

260

You arrange an evening with a friend, but on the day before, an unexpected chance to do something much more exciting comes up. How would you handle the situation?

261

What is your biggest disappointment in life? your biggest failure? Has anything positive come out of them?

262

If computers could think and feel, should people be able to own them? How—if at all—should people be punished for hurting or destroying such machines?

■ Would it be murder to obliterate the memory of a conscious computer? What if it were fully backed up?

263

How do you think you'd react if you found that you weren't the product of a random meeting of sperm and egg, but had been selected by your parents from 100 of their embryos because of your likely traits and temperament?

264

If you could pass your life slumbering peacefully, cared for in every way, entranced by marvelous, wonderful dreams, would you? Why?

265

If a foreign country embarked on a eugenics program to raise the average IQ of their next generation of children by 30 points, so that average kids there were smarter than 49 out of 50 kids here, how would you want our country to respond?

■ How might such an effort change your attitudes about human enhancement?

If you were hypnotized to make your biggest worry fade away, how would your life change? What is that worry?

267

Do you do more listening or talking? Might it be good for you to shift that balance?

■ What are you looking for when you interact with people? Does what you discuss and how you do it typically lead in that direction? If not, what could you do that might serve you better?

268

If you could return to any previous point in your life, change a decision you made, and pick up from there (obliterating everything that has happened to you since then), would you? If so, would you like to retain the memory of the life you are giving up even though you could never recapture it?

269

Do you enjoy sleeping in physical contact with your lover?

Would you commit perjury for a close friend? For example, might you testify that your best friend was driving carefully when he hit a pedestrian even though he actually was laughing at something on the radio and not paying attention?

If you won a housekeeping robot that could do every household task from picking up your clothes to shopping for food and cooking dinner, what would you still want to do yourself?

272

Relative to the population at large, how do you rate your integrity? your openness? your warmth?

■ Do you think your family would agree with you?

273

Five years from now, what would you like to be doing? What do you think you will be doing?

■ Is your life turning out better or worse than you thought it might 5 years ago? In what ways?

If you learned that a century ago your great-great-grandfather robbed and murdered someone, would you try to make it up to their now-distant offspring? What if the great-great-grandson of the victim came to you and demanded that you or your kids pay his kids $10,000 to make up for what your ancestor did?

■ Should you be held accountable for something—be it slavery, genocide, or some other historical injustice—that you have no connection to except by being of the same religion, nationality, or ethnicity as the wrongdoers? If so, how many generations back should such responsibility extend? If not, would it matter if you had benefited indirectly from the wrong?

275

If you could prevent one of the following, which would you choose: an earthquake in Chile that would kill 40,000 people, a plane crash at your local airport that would kill 200 people, or an automobile accident that would kill a friend of yours?

276

Do you often find yourself—just to be polite—saying things you don't mean? For example, when you say good-bye to people who bore you, do you pretend to have enjoyed their company?

If you could put a near-perfect lie detector on your phone to flag any dishonesties, would you? If so, would you use it a lot or just for very specific conversations?

■ Do you think we'd be better or worse off if we always knew when we were being deceived? How might society be different if everyone had to tell the truth all the time?

278

If you came upon the scene of a terrible highway accident just after the ambulances arrived, and your presence would neither help nor hinder anyone, would you stop to watch?

If you thought that being cryonically frozen after you died would give you a chance of being brought back to life in a century or two, would you choose that instead of burial or cremation? Assume the costs were identical. If not, why not?

If you had to tattoo your arm with a message to yourself, what would you write?

281

If the car you were buying for your teen-ager offered an option to continuously monitor the vehicle's status and location so that you could see where he was and how he was driving, would you?

■ Would you agree to have such a feature on your own car?

282

While running on an icy sidewalk in front of a neighbor's house, you slip and break your leg. Would you sue your neighbor if you stood to make a lot of money?

283

If you could choose the manner of your death, what would it be?

■ Would you rather die a hero's death trying to save someone, go quietly with your friends around you, or just pass away in your sleep?

■ In what ways do your feelings about death reflect the way you live your life?

284

What would you do if you came home unexpectedly one afternoon and found your spouse, or partner, on the Internet engaged in steamy online role-playing with a cyber-lover? Assume they'd been doing it for months, but had never discussed meeting physically.

How would a betrayal like this compare to a real-world one-night stand?

285

Do you trust your intuition? What important decisions in your professional life have you based largely upon intuition? What about in your personal life?

Would you like to be president of the United States? Why? What if you knew that 1 in 4 people would despise you by the time you left office?

Would you take a pill that, without side effects, made you feel utterly fulfilled for a year—glad just to be you, doing whatever you already do? Would you choose differently if you knew the effect would be permanent?

■ Do you think that having a deep, enduring feeling of fulfillment about what you are presently doing would enhance or diminish your life? In what ways might such feelings alter your current relationships?

288

Do you view government more as a force for good that should be expanded or as a necessary evil that should be reduced?

Have you had any personal experiences that suggest that the opposite might be closer to the truth?

289

If the military could guide a hummingbird-sized drone through virtually any window in the world and explode it, would you want it used for assassination? If so, who'd be at the top of your list?

290

Do you look to the future more with anticipation or anxiety?

291

If you were guaranteed honest responses to any three questions, whom would you question and what would you ask?

ACKNOWLEDGMENTS

I want to thank Maisie Tivnan, my editor, who brought a fresh perspective to many of the questions and was always a pleasure to work with; Joe Spieler, my longtime agent and friend, who made numerous trenchant comments that kept me on my toes; and Lori Fish, my wife, who has had to put up with more questions than she thought she'd ever endure in one lifetime.

I also want to thank several others who offered helpful comments and suggestions on early drafts of the manuscript, in particular Talia Mata, Susan Bolotin, Julio Gagné, Deborah Patton, Carlos Devis, and Robert Mogel.

And I want to thank Peter Workman for patiently tolerating so many delays in bringing this material into being, and Carolan Workman for her love of questions and her key role in making the project happen.

Finally, I want to again thank those who played a meaningful part in the first edition: John Summer, Michael Cader, David Breznau, Claudia Summer, Don Ponturo, Libby Anderson, Richard Campbell, Ann Cole, Ginny Mazur, Peter Trent, Fred Weber, and Arshad Zakaria. Without their early help, this new edition would not exist. Two of these friends were particularly important as I returned to questioning and began to pull together the new edition: Don Ponturo, who encouraged me in my new effort and helped with the book's tone; and John Summer, a fellow questioner since my college days, who contributed so much to the earlier question books that his presence is indelibly embedded in the pages of this work as well.

ABOUT THE AUTHOR

Questions are Dr. Gregory Stock's passion. He started asking them as a child and never stopped. His question books—including *The Kids' Book of Questions* and *Love & Sex: The Book of Questions*—are miniclassics that have sold more than 4 million copies and have been translated into 18 languages.

He has a Ph.D. from Johns Hopkins and an MBA from Harvard. He serves on the California Advisory Committee on Stem Cells and Cloning and on the editorial boards of the *Journal of Evolution & Technology* and *Rejuvenation Research*. Stock has written more than 60 papers and 3 influential books on technology, ethics, and public policy in the life sciences: *Engineering the Human Germline*; *Metaman: The Merging of Humans and Machines into a Global Superorganism*; and *Redesigning*

299

Humans: Our Inevitable Genetic Future, which won the Kistler Book Prize for science books.

Stock has made more than 1,000 media appearances to discuss questions and values, and he frequently appears on TV and radio as an authority on the implications of genomics and other technologies. He was the founding director of the Program on Medicine, Technology & Society at the UCLA School of Medicine and founding CEO of both Signum Biosciences, which is developing therapeutics for Alzheimer's, and Ecoeos, which has a genetic test to gauge personal vulnerability to mercury exposure. His website is gregorystock.net.